SECOND NATURE

Second Nature

PATRICIA CARLIN

Poems

MARSH HAWK PRESS · NEW YORK · 2017

First Edition

2 4 6 8 9 7 5 3 1

Marsh Hawk Press books are published by Marsh Hawk Press, Inc.,
a not-for-profit corporation under section 501 (c) 3
United States Internal Revenue Code

LIBRARY OF CONGRESS CATALOGING-IN-PUBLICATION DATA

Names: Carlin, Patricia L., author.
Title: Second nature / Patricia Carlin.
Description: East Rockaway, New York : Marsh Hawk Press, 2016.
Identifiers: LCCN 2016030414 | ISBN 9780996427555 (pbk.)
Classification: LCC PS3603.A7525 A6 2016 | DDC 811/.6--dc23 LC record available at
https://lccn.loc.gov/2016030414

Design and typesetting by Mark Melnick
Set in Verdigris MVB Pro (text) and Domaine (headings)

Publication of this book was supported in part by a generous grant from the
Community of Literary Magazines and Presses via the
New York State Council on the Arts

MARSH HAWK PRESS
P.O. Box 206, East Rockaway, New York 11518-0206
www.marshhawkpress.org

For Roy, always.
And for Daniel, Katie, and Sylvie.

CONTENTS

SECTION THREE

SECTION ONE

Heading Home

Leaving our cities for unknown ports.
Losing our papers, and paper itself
born of leaves and dirt.
No moon to light the corners.
No music sifting through trees.
Homes on the rocks, towns receding, forests
spreading their green light,
and the tax collector hovering.

What works on paper
dissolves in a salt sea—or birdbath—or bathtub—
or, even, a pool of rainwater.
That too will work,
and the words of knowing
can return to the comfortable darkness.
There are trees, snow, mountains
to walk with us into the paper-free night
where presidents live / and all of us, too.
What to call home, the scenery we feed on?
Fields clipped of their cattle.
Moods and light
equally unfamiliar.

Bad Angel

Chain me up,
    bad angel
on this straight road
    of no labels.
Your separate words
    are indoor activities—
finite,
    happy.
Put some dumb jokes
    and no pity
into this mouth.

[on a day in December]

On a day in December, packed with calm gestures, staring ahead at the non-working television, I came for the first time skin to skin with my own contagions. Paying nothing, taking everything—even dirt, even the least sky, distant and useless.

But I did understand. I was kicked awake by what filled in the blanks—misdirections—wrong roads. I knew the new wouldn't get old if it just kept coming. There was no "on the other hand"—just noise, noise, and whatever's brewing in the fog light of consciousness. Looking for a solid body. Lying down with water.

Elsewhere, Always

Years slid along.
Twilight ahead, twilight behind.
Here, there are only moods.

Light bearing down: another hot morning.
Uptown
throws its cold shadow backward.

I don't know—will never know—
how little
my own thoughts stick to each other.
How they are public, in spite of my wishes,
because they will ring out
over the silent city
looking for more silence.

Can our lives matter
to anyone looking on from a distance?

The smallest action
can usher in empires.
But this is our only landscape.
Nothing is central:
not ripe peaches, or city sunsets,
or the hills with their unknown names.

Half-flooded shores,
thinning suburbs
mixing with pride
on shadowy lawns.

Alternate Universe

"If you come to a fork in the road, take it."
—YOGI BERRA

They're nothing, too puny, too few—those gone-beyond-finding mothers, brothers. They lie down in deep grass, claiming wildness, poisoned with tameness. The air is their cage, water their blind alleys, always circling back. You who live on land, that's nothing too, the nothing between sky and the black roots underground. They can't live there, and neither can you.

We argue about water and wind—we switch sides. You fly, I swim. No sieve to catch that slow seeping. It's not blood, just whatever trickles away and is never exhausted, never over. Tiny domestic drains—sink, bathtub, water swirling against the clock. Impossibly distant poles are leaving no choice. Bore through the earth to the other side, where water shifts direction. With the clock or against it—nothing changes.

Once, she began, a girl lived happily in the not-forever-after. One morning was the morning before, then the missing after. But that unhappened. The angel of yesterday swooped down and slashed tomorrow in two. Now there were two girls, the one who lived happily in the ever-after and the one who didn't. That can happen for you, too. Open your arms to the black angel— die to your old life. Someone else will live that life, someone who once was you. Let her not imagine that forking path. It will be too bitter—better to live out her bent life in the other after. It too was a way to go.

After Noon

It was noon by the clock,
but I lacked
ways to alter that. The promised tools
never arrived. And yes, I was afraid
of seeming to care too much, of letting
anything out. But really, I knew
that what I wanted
was already missing. Stolen—
trolls at work—ha ha, no such thing!
Then where did everything go?

The noon whistle sounded at 12:03 exactly.
All the machines were running, but the operators
were gone for the night.
Pushing my way through crowds, I was happy
to be padding along. Finishing first,
last, somewhere in the middle—I didn't care—
just glad to outrun
all my sad captains, happiness growing
like grass in the parking lot
of a paved-over city. Oh sure, you'll say,
we're all in the same leaky boat.
Well, I'm not. I remember
greener grasses. Lilies, floating. The cool
delicate feet of a salamander.

Not the door of a dream—those are mostly over—
and a good thing, too. Who wants to encounter
deep pools, rockslides, falling through air,
when you can be a grown-up, and get
just where you always hoped you would?

Let's get out of here.
These blue fluorescent lights
are depressing me.
Of course day is growing darker—
that's only natural.
And here comes our kind duplicitous nurse
to enfold us in soft covers. So glad
to come out in paperback,
waiting to see what our readers think of us.
Shall we think of them, too?

Nowhere Men

who lived in the world's long messages.

Two by two, alone.

Who, for years of a half-life

were silent.

Who stood on broken ground.

who stepped and stepped, but went

Nowhere.

Wires and gauze shrouded them,

hunger held them,

want netted them.

Question after question. / But in the dark

voices were muffled

as if it took light

to hear

a heart's deep lies.

Islands of

no less than hatreds, disaffection
here waiting to speak
wordlessly.

A year? A minute?
cranking down its own sad pole.

Taste. Touch. One body rubbing against another
in the cloud bed,
honey and salt on the tongue, young and young,
half dreamt,
half felt,
nothing forgotten, and more, more
for the hardened heart of the bent world.

All sight
believes in the light that sight was made for.
Useless light,
blind to the hour.

My pure self
who does not love, who is not loved.
Before this life we were together
and never now again.

If You Call That Love

Far out at sea, I looked
toward the elusive coast.
Would it appear before evening?
Would I love
the swamps, ragged palm trees, crabs
clattering their pincers
over the black volcanic beach?

If you call that love. I do, because, after all,
there'd be something, not nothing,
in all the remembered ice of a life gone missing.

I did not love those days, till age said, wait,
the ritual of morning
will always see you through. It will replace
the cold beautiful moon
hanging low
in the eastern sky.

Earlier, there was only myself. I hadn't seen
all those doubles coming along
though I always understood
that the moon would double and triple
like all my friends.

What I loved
was the crowd closing in—
my look-alikes, which weren't, really.
It's land that's important, anyhow,
whichever island you happen to reach.
One is as good as another.
To prefer hibiscus—or walruses—or bubbling pools of lava
is perfectly pointless.

Soon land will loom up, and I'll disembark,
waving goodbye
to the ship that carried me there.
So glad I never encountered
lurking pirates, whirlpool gulfs.
This is a better
point of departure.

SECTION TWO

This Fall

the sky is not falling.
But look, in the corner
something unwelcome.
Nothing spoiled—nothing running amok—
just hard to believe
that all that leaking green
could ever be blotted up.
Not to worry. The protocol will save us.
Just wash, wash again, and look out—
a fern over here, a bear there, and leaves
leaving for better things.
They junked all that green,
and you can, too.

GPS

"Where are your times?" he sang near the band mates of tune at Joe's pub on Tuesday question, and then answered it himself. "Your moment is nowhere but here." He didn't mean to seem pushy, really. The distance was about the people of two comforts bridging their emotional direction and finding each other in position. "I know where you are, and I know that I am here," Mr. Mota offered later in the question, his nights trailing behind him. "That I am here," he sang again, several shows beyond.

It Was Dark When You Left

after BARBARA GUEST

Nothing restrained you. You tried to come back but there were no doors, just forgetfulness. I've lost the chain. My dog is gone, my dog with the one gold tooth. And there were never any doves.

Do not forget me. I'll be climbing an iron staircase down in the dark. There will be no castles, no cliffs, no pears or illusions.

Your letters will allow me everything, tell me nothing. Because you are combing your long hair, leaning out of the silver tower and blowing me kisses. This minute is calling, but you are gone and there's no one to hear.

So Late in the Promises

In the blaze of just sitting around,
trees, grass, windows are hard at work,
melting all the moons
to one imagination—a disappearing stone
in the river of days.

The great streetlamps are erasing evening.
Crowds and glass cross over the river,
receding in orderly rows.
And that's it for flowers and yards.

Only the cold work of forgetting
is left for the streetlamps.
Tables, chairs, rooms and their shadows
blink out with the light.
No more crowds. And no evenings.
Now what. Days of forgetting
everywhere?

Exacto Knife

Meet him coming home
with his black bag. Someone
should meet him, and there's only you.
He doesn't hear.

But you can hear.
You know the sound
his key makes in the lock—
can greet his never-again

arrival
with never-again children and wife—and always
straining backwards to hear
words gone by on the track

of yesterday. Whistles, clatters, twenty black books
in a white bookcase. The North wind
blows through the pages. Her
other name is death—kind death. She

blows through the years.
Her long black hair wraps around you.
She's trying to tell you something,
but it's too late—you're too fast—the blast

through the chink in the attic fades
as you skim through the years.
Time for the knife.
Red beads

well up on your skin.
There's nothing under that skin.
All clear as glass
though you are swaddled in thirty thick coats

of not beginning.
Put one foot
in front of the other.
See where you get.

Time Travel

What's in anyone's head
means nothing. Space
is the light of nothing
is an eye to see

a box of shadows
needing translation.
You think meaning
is in the difference?

That's where leaving
begins / the space
where light trickles over the roofs of before
spectral and distant.

There were flowers, and girls,
and workmen,
tools hanging heavy from their belts.
(No mixing, though.)

Form of what's gone,

a rake combing the red fields
for rhythms, for faces, hearts,
lungs—time
to pay back all you took,

to lie down in the dirt,

plant your body in the red rows

reading scars as stars,

furrows as fertile cuts.

The Original Can Not Be Found

He said, "The Goth master hammer
slams
Constantine's marble toe."

She said, "Words are always trying to make ruin
instruct us."

He said, "The master of the wall speaks
a simpler language.
Bluestone. Limestone. Shale."

She said, "A body walks through fire
stripped raw."

O brief alphabet
framed by that stone day.

Didn't Appear,

the woman at the center. Sour swaying
against names, finding no body,
just mind with its watery sway.
From syncope to
nothing repeated,
not even the same dreams.
Well, what did you expect?
He loved his wife, called her
"honey" and "sweetheart" and "wifey."
But she stepped through the net of his names,
found always elsewhere
in a flash of headlights—not a stricken deer
but a slowly padding opossum,
somehow eluding
the oncoming car. Splayed pink feet.
Naked prehensile tail.

City Limits

You try to turn off the lights
in the city of small grievances.
It's a tourist trap, all schlock and glitz,
flashing eat me, drink me, see, stay,
touch these bodies,
walk those streets.

This city is full.
Lights burn in the night, bodies blaze.
It's hard to breathe, yes,
but never alone
in the city of small grievances.
Once you loved the man
whose touch still satisfies,
and that is enough.

2. BE LESS THAN YOU CAN

Then, outside the shallow
city of small things,
slam the door shut.
Don't pronounce, don't claim.
Tie up whatever you don't know
in stale words, half whispers.
Loud obvious music
leads to nothing,
to nowhere,
to a low country of dust and forgetting
under a shrunken sky.

All Night Long

All night long
against air, against nothing.
Pools of pools
beyond which
there are no blue leaks,
no names of words.
Incurable questions:
Whose street? Whose face?
What if a kettle, a seam, a song?
Speed without purpose,
laws without action
as if nothing were left
at the white white core
of zero.

In the Ditches of Daylight

He directed the droplets, made do with the broken stream,
then mapped the field of his body, laid out its borders.
Night withdrew its betrayals. Darkness erased all broken promises.
There was no time for dalliance. No time for new routines.

For a few, a shrinking cohort,
bound together by weakening strands, braided by accidents,
remembering meant forgetting.
In the shallow ditch of morning
light balked at the highway entrance, said no
to whatever might lie
down the rejected road. What the wind refused,
what the little breeze kept to itself.

There's no point in planning.
The long light will go down, the line
between day and night slip slowly into darkness,
and darkness climb toward forgotten
glimmers of morning light.

[in the last hours of night]

In the last hours of night I said,
No new books. Of making many books
there's no end—and there's nothing new anyway
under the waning sun.

In my cold bed
I saw the animals
turning their backs. Of course they did.
They own without payment the shining wordless world.

I couldn't make myself wake
or sleep. Had to make up dreams.
The world hadn't changed—I had.
Too much looking sideways.

Is it good, I asked, to stare head-on
at the finally unknown world?
To say, and say again,
"There's no true loss"
as if meaning it, and meaning itself
were slipping slowly
down a whitening slope
toward a long lingering radiant sunset.

Up Here

no time you can count in minutes.
Out of that bedrock, nothing.
And there's no pleasure
in looking down from 30,000 feet.
Yet people are never quiet. They kick
choice in the teeth,
grab the old, pretend its new. But
there's nothing new
under the lax sky.
And there's no balloon
to carry you silently over the known world.

In the world under the world
they're calling for blood.
Let them have it.
You've come all this way
to listen.
The moon rounding the blackest river
sends its borrowed light
to the far shore. Mother, father
whose speech I will one day learn.
All night
you lie in your black beds.
Your voices reach for the sun.
You were the sun.

from Lives of the Painters

The door open, he painted
the given.

No, there was no grass.
Burnt dreams.
Borrowed stars.

All day, and
little pictures.

The Story of Quietude

People do not understand
the river of living
as it narrows, and cities fall away
growing lighter, airier, closer to "real life".

They enter a room
where the towers fall backward,
story by story,
so they can rise again.

Nothing is said aloud.

You are here, and so
I will tell you everything.
Somewhere, someone is disappearing
through days and nights.

Let's not talk anymore.
Let's just appreciate
us, our plywood fort,
this solid silent air.

I'll Never Ask the Houses

where I'm going, the bright houses
far from corrupted air.
Nowhere you'd risk—everywhere.
The difference is death,
or maybe it's just
useless instruction.

We love the dead, discredit the living.
"The dead." What is that?

I'm a bare bringer of death,
my own widow.
Who sends me cards? Letters?
Home news, gone.

Time pretends it's gravity,
always pulling down—
but it's a breeze, too.
Riding the updraft, grabbing air,
that's what air is for.
For example, there is not nothing, now.
I think your arms are where I might go
if I were not always sailing upwards
into bluer air,
each cloud a station
looking down on the tiny globe.

And that's a comfort. To know that everything falls
and is gone
with less than the speed of light.

Words become worlds.
I'll speak before I leap, look before I sleep.

SECTION THREE

3:00 A.M.

Terror. 10,000 frets.
That cartoon I don't want to be,
some sad sack crying in a river,
drowning in it. This leaf,
that stone, the least stick
more interesting
than all that tiresome moaning.

Let night
settle gently around you.
Stroke her soft blackness.
Don't wish for the moon
to float you
out of this wakeful night.
Look to (reach for) the pitiless sun.
So many mournings
gone with the light.

As If

the names

were salt on the tongue, grief's

way back.

not this or that,

but the whole length.

uneven beds,

sleep to sleep—

all the little ways

white-fingered dawn tries

to cancel night.

maybe nothing but.

Live elsewhere.

Lie down with night and call it day.

here is the trail of a thousand years—

your steps

can't wear it out.

Every Cell New Again

Because it is not that face:
backward, heavy,
a desert of beginning.

I thought, All this is only time.

Laura sleeping without a leaf.
Sunlight, shade,
From glass into years, years into morning.

This is not the body I will die in.

A Child's Train

crosses
the imagined river
high on its iron trestle.
Twenty years? Fifty years?

And where? Do not suppose
the track split.
"If" is not the doorway back.
There is no doorway back.

A body enters the world
through its mother's tunnel
at whose glimmering end
the light of the slippery world calls out.

No matter.
There's the open field.
Here is the script
you wrote for you.

The way out is over the wall. Easy.
Eighty steps
and into the wavering landscape
yellow with tall grasses.

It's endless
as the little train's imagined journey
over its high black iron trestle
and home to the waiting station.

Keeping Time

The living are gracious.
On the great dial
they step to the sun.
Truth is on fire, and all our planets
conspire with light.

But look, people are erased.
Home turns up only disorder and sleep.

That statement lies.
The beyond was given up—
the long principle
carved from art, sea, land.

What could be sadder?
You tell me—
Crossings? A flooded port
calling for air?

Trapped in intent,
a breathing heart
has no time to return.

Aluminum minutes flash by.

First Love

Phillis is glad to be captured looking dewy-eyed and open. Always open.

She is skateboarding down Fifth Avenue, missing her first love: his rimless
glasses, his three-piece suits, his gold pocket watch tucked into his
vest pocket.

Phillis is sad—she wants to try again. Lay her down in Marbletown.

Time to spread Phillis around.

Thinking My Way Out
of a Paper Bag

There is a tide in the affairs of men
that taken at the flood, leads on to fortune.
　　—SHAKESPEARE

No more trumpet bray,
blare, scare tactics
for winds and bags.

No more With or
Against, Black or
White.

Confusion
rains over shining seas,
flooded plains.

(O Captain, O Presidente.
We are sad.
we are scared.
We are not very pretty, most of us, and
not very rich.
Less rich now.)

Sweet country.

(Meltdown. Bears on their ice floes, rats in their bayous.)

All systems set to go.
Our little lives are rounded with an O.

In *Starting Today: 100 Poems for Obama's First 100 Days*

Square of Sense

Goodbye, my love.
        You never wavered.

Cover me. Stand over.
           Before

was nothing.   And soon will be.

Shelve of love—
Who cares?

What's underneath is never over.

   Stand fast and over me.

After is over

And there is nowhere
as any the most precious square of sense.

An Old World

An old world
saying *new, new*

beginning
in the long hall of the body.

Some girl became my mother.
I became someone's mother.

You who I love,
how many lives can we lead together?

This night
I'll find out the urgent

gates of the body.
How we're dispossessed.

Familiar uncoupling.
Turn to find

whatever our history razed,
and raised.

All Reports

are the same—
they didn't fall.
Unbreached cities,
intact bodies.

But there's the little needle
slowly pricking out
reds, blues, blacks
on willing flesh.

You must not forget.

You will not remember.

More Questions

A fertile natural sea.
Inland songs, springs of time—
a last curve.
Land always just ahead,
over the next curve.

Duty. Vision. Too grand,
all of it. Grandiose.
What was she thinking?
Out of ideas, out of words.
No one left. What's
black against the paper over there?
Is it hers? Does she owe or own it?

Oh, the great relaxed month of examples:
A forgotten way.
A dropped vacation.
Gulls once heard that flew over cornfields
too far from the sea.

Not Night

It's not natural. Not night,
the hole inside the hole.
This way, that way.
No way.
Can you keep going?
The sun keeps going.
Old, young,
taking your footsteps.
Tomorrow someone will ask,
"Is this what she wanted?"
And someone will answer
"She passed this way
under the weightless wash of sky."

SECTION FOUR

Finding Silence

after W. S. MERWIN

Voices leave and do not come back.
Yet the words remember.

They know now
that day is glass.

The words are young.
What is old is the dark repeating.

We are phrases and children
in the verbs of the new trees.

Rising Moon

That day the sun ambled across the sky.
Rain
fell on forgotten streets, and
on graves in green valleys.
Hers. Her husband's. Trees
at the edge of
lawns, still waters. The moon
rising over all the makers
making
black tracks across white paper. Tracks for the

wind to read, the rising
moon to make sense of.

Work

I've kept a calendar,
declared my body irrevocable.
Bowed before some things,
was pious to nothing. Hands
were the order. From my gestures
my words arose. From my bed
I greeted my sheets. Keys
took on a deeper music.
The peace of my books
was the seasons' loss.

Walking All Night

A safely dead father, sculpted by time,
whose hands divide the distance

That black thing
is the bread of his hand

"muddy worlds"—"longing"—"night," because
"light" is too full of distance

My childhood elegy
for what that meant, with its island words

A willow by a river
is meaning to someone

I remembered grief:
how absence

disabled
all the luminous structures

of air

"The Wise Man [or Woman]"

"Se þonne þisne . . .   wise geþohte
ond þis deorce lif   deope geondþenceð"
        —OLD ENGLISH, FROM "THE WANDERER"

"He who on this . . .   wisely thinks
And this dark life   deeply ponders"

Snow scattering, following rumors
that winter's death is just down the road.
Faces rising
like leaves going back to their trees—
winter to fall, fall to summer—drawn upward
by wishing. Bare afternoons. Houses cracking
under the weight of remembered snow.
None are for sale. No one is buying.
Buyers are gone
wherever the wind went.

Windows slam shut, like widows, or stones.
Grass grows deep down / into the ground.
Its green light
shoots upward—a shadow lawn.
No one walks there.
The dogs of yesteryear
have padded happily into their lost reflections.

The world is full of itself. No use to tell it anything.
A wise man or woman thinks deeply on the dark
while snow rages
somewhere off camera.

This world
is a drawer stuffed with the junk of years.
Someone else
will have to go through it.

[will be the real]

will be the real
  darkness or sleeper
will be even
  the odd winnowing
will be a minute, will be a year,
  will be the flat world's edge

The world is prose. Every thing is its own reason. This table hard in its oak grain. That plain glass window lit by the sun of the whole world. My dead brother's steel knife. Sharpness, hardness, cuts, scraping—how real and loved you were/are. I'll follow soon where we'll never meet. Now was the time to meet, and leaving is its own raw end.

The Naturalist Looks Back

as she walks,

brushing against Nature.

Coasts, ships, a traveler

holding to her coastline.

She sees

different islands, different eggs.

Different expressions call

from different trees.

After all those islands of archipelagoes

all she can see

is growing smaller.

Her grappling hooks depart

bound for an island

where no orchard has a moon.

Second Nature

Copies some thing,
maybe. A fluid decade
thick with colored streaks,
and some body calling, "I am not
a machine."
Whose body?
Exactly how many did you say?

Into the scrofulous world, garden forgotten,
color is slashing its own bright way.

•

There is no soul, you said.
A living city blackens its sun
and the tulips are so over.
There are still green firs and silver birches
whining for snow. Rising over the glimmering ground
stars pretend
they are winking out.

As if they didn't know they were suns!
I hate the weight of what I know:
in the sound house
made of night and fake stars
there's no master maker.
Bury the walls.
Let the evergreens and the silver birches cover them up.

•

The moon is a truth-teller.
Don't let the lying sun
pretend it's showing you morning.
Stick with the shivery moon.
Your body
is a bed for all seasons.
The moon will lie in it.

Acknowledgments

For a life in poetry, and the life that makes poetry possible, I am grateful beyond measure to my colleagues and students at The New School; to Jennifer and Donald Mathis, John Carlin and Sarah Newman, and Shepard and Merriem Palitz; to poets Jeanne Marie Beaumont, Sharon Dolin, Elaine Equi, Phillis Levin, Marie Ponsot, Anna Rabinowitz, and Alex Silberman; and to Donna Silberberg, Mary Beth Rose, Anne Donovan Rosivach, and Lynn Hazlewood. Finally, my thanks to Sandy McIntosh for his wise shepherding of this book and of Marsh Hawk Press; and to Thomas Fink, whose scrupulous and inspired editing made this a better book.

Poems in this book work incrementally as parts of a whole, and many appear here for the first time. Thanks to the editors of the anthologies and journals who have published versions of some of these poems: *The Traveler's Vade Mecum*, ed. Helen Klein Ross (Red Hen Press, 2016); *Starting Today: Poems for Obama's First Hundred Days*, ed. Rachel Zucker and Arielle Greenberg (The University of Iowa Press, 2010); *The Manhattan Review*; and *Marsh Hawk Review*.

About the author

Patricia Carlin's books include *Quantum Jitters* and *Original Green* (poems), and *Shakespeare's Mortal Men* (prose). She has published widely in journals and anthologies, and she has received fellowships from The MacDowell Colony and VCCA. She teaches literature and poetry writing at The New School, and she co-edits the poetry journal *Barrow Street*.